The Avalanche
and the
Executor

The final rest of a friend and the avalanche of events

B. J. Doyle

Produced by:

FriesenPress
Suite 300 – 852 Fort Street
Victoria, BC, Canada V8W 1H8

www.friesenpress.com

Distributed to the trade by The Ingram Book Company

Acknowledgements:
Special thanks to Tim, Ray, David, Lynne, Bonnie family and friends whose encouragement and support cleared the way after the avalanche.

B. Doyle writes from the heart. This informative & poignant book provides a glimpse of dear friends as they cope with end of life planning. She gives the reader an insight into the emotional aspects as well as practical information on the legal implications of dealing with the loss of a loved one. A must read.

~ Joanne Robertson. B.A. B.S.W.

This book is an excellent resource for anyone planning to write a will. The author presents a number of points that I did not think of in my own preparations. What could be a very dry subject is presented with humour and imagination.

~ D. Doyle B.Sc. M. Sc.

A totally unique experience of a fasinating story woven with practical information.

~ R. Cinel. B. Ed.

Table of Contents

Preface

It is surprising how many people both young and old do not have a valid will. These same individuals have an estate; some even have children they provide for. When I asked them why they had never planned for death the answers were numerous.

Three reasons did emerge as a common excuse:

1. They assumed their estate could be divided easily and clearly by the remaining family members, with no complications.

2. They didn't know how to write a will and they didn't have a lawyer who could help them.

3. They had no idea who would actually take on the responsibility of administering the estate after their death.

This story is about two friends who decide to prepare for the death of one of them. They proceed with the will and determine what steps the executor will take when the time comes.

Sami is twenty four years older than Buddy. The age discrepancy does not matter to them. They share the same passion for being out in the wilderness, so they see each other almost daily to explore ski trails they groom through the forest.

They share their private thoughts and emotions when skiing. Buddy records their discussions, shedding light on events that take place much later in the year.

As time goes on, it becomes evident that Sami's health is failing. He decides to prepare his executor Buddy for the administration of his estate. Neither of them had handled an estate before, but they are sure they can do it. What they don't know are the estate laws. They begin to plan and organize Sami's affairs, with an eye toward his demise.

Steps for the administration of the estate are written down. Bankers, lawyers and even a funeral home are picked. Their careful preparations are only the start of what becomes an arduous journey. A mix up in Sami's financial affairs creates problems for Buddy.

Once Sami is gone, Buddy is faced with the enormous task of cancelling Sami's life, stopping pensions, paying medical costs, obtaining refunds to add to the estate and more.

Buddy comes up against the one member of the family who decides to interfere with the administration process; every family has one. Through his grief, Buddy processes the estate, step by step. This is not fast enough for family members awaiting their inheritance. There is a process that takes time and must be followed.

Trust in each other's ability to provide the right information and loyalty to each other was the foundation of the relationship between Sami and Buddy. These characteristics that served the friends so well are tested after the death of Sami. Buddy comes up against questions that have to be addressed. The answers are not easy to find; this should not be the case but often happens when money is involved. What follows is Buddy's telling of how it all unfolded.

The Avalanche
and the
Executor

An Avalanche to Plan For

Sami nicknamed me Buddy when I was very young. He was my mentor. Though evident to me now, he didn't seem to be guiding me through the changing seasons at the time. Like a bull moose, he appeared strong and in charge; I followed along. Here is an account of our travels together and some of the lessons I've learned.

Growing up in the mountains was great fun, educational and every day was an adventure with no end in sight. I learned the beauty of the wilderness, was taught to observe animals (not the human kind) and to watch the seasons come and go. There are four seasons for a reason. The birth, growth and development of most things happen in the spring. Newborn animals appear clumsy and uncoordinated, but precious and cute. This might be a stretch when looking at a moose calf. A moose cow is very protective of this long legged big nosed offspring – they have the potential of power and dominance.

Spring is a time of new beginnings: viridian greens of moss and grass carpet the forest floor; delicate violet crocus stretch up before the white daisies; Indian paintbrushes and brown eyed susans; wild rose bushes bud out and bloom. It is a magical time, full of promise. Many animals have their young. The moose will calve at this time and the young will stay with the mother for one year. The fresh spring air is filled with the chirping of returning birds and the rustle of furry feet. It begs those who use the forest to protect and nurture it to maturity.

Moose have four distinct territories influenced by the seasons. They plan and move in preparation for birth in spring. The heat in summer moves them again to low lying cool moist areas. They move back to the dry ground under the colorful canopy of the forest in the fall, and finally seek shelter in the dense warm forest during the cold winter months.

Human babies are also highly protected. Their growth and development are shaped by the parents and the environment. The best directions and encouragements are meant to last a lifetime. Young children start to accumulate possessions before they can appreciate their wealth. As the summer of life approaches, the newborn develops, and eventually, an adult productive phase takes over.

An estate starts with a small serviceable home, perhaps some savings and great promise. The collection expands over a lifetime. A fresh look at the accumulation usually means an evaluation of the spoils is necessary.

Foundations of grandeur, like a mature forest, are sometimes met if the person takes care of their accumulated wealth; however, sometimes they fall short. Maturity is often measured in beauty, strength and wealth. Wisdom is encouraged but the learning curve is steep. Success can be an absolute measure, the results only knowable after the final season.

A documented assessment of a person's belongings becomes a measurement for the estate. A will made by the parent/friend should stipulate who will benefit from the estate. If there are specific items for one individual or group, the will must stipulate those be exempt from the bulk of the accumulation.

Fall can be a colorful scramble before the branches shed, while other vegetation remains untouched. Sorting, selecting and assessment fill the days of the animals and birds during the cool days. The cold nights mark the coming of winter. The rains come. A gathering of resources in preparation for winter continues to occur.

Downsizing, sorting, donating, repairing or replacing assets are integral steps of preparing before the writing of a will.

The winter season holds unparalleled beauty. Hoar frost paints intricate patterns on the foliage, based on the wind direction. Icicles acting as prisms form, drip, freeze and grow, spiralling downward. The first signs of cold dark short days are ahead. Light snow, full of water crystals that light up like diamonds during brief periods of sun fall on the forest. A sense of urgency creeps into the preparations. Storage, repair and hibernation sites are sought. Snow eventually starts to build; the sun comes weakly and infrequently. Layer upon layer of ice and snow start to accumulate in the high country.

Lists, files, names of contact people must be made in the preparations. Information will accumulate and just when you think you have thought of everything it becomes evident more paperwork is required.

Nature was in a delicate balance until winter's avalanche season. An avalanche is an accumulation of "stuff" that eventually unleashes into a traumatic event. The balance of nature can quickly be altered by the slide. Mountain dwellers watch the white snow build above them, plan escape routes and take care to dodge the slide.

We don't all live in the mountains, yet similar events can unleash an avalanche of a different variety.

Written plans and preparation are tasks many avoid altogether, or only just get started without completion. Yet, this major event will happen to you; you will die. Everyone does, and your preparation now determines how big or small the slide bearing down on your Executor.

The cold winter air is a reminder of the inevitable road to death. The quick change of seasons can mirror the speed of life. Change surprises most of us and while we can't predict the exact end, we know it will come. Just as the dreaded winter avalanche looms above, our unorganized affairs threaten to engulf our executor.

Many would think their avalanche is far away; "time" is on their side. This maybe true, but to do it right one does need that time to prepare, plan, reflect and prepare some more.

Death is the event; the avalanche occurs after the probate of the will. The executor will have a myriad of duties before the estate can be finalized. Preparation is necessary to prevent the catastrophic destruction of family or friends that can occur over possessions.

If you teach yourself now, as I was taught by Sami, and act on what you've learned, the memory of your contributions during your lifetime will be appreciated like mountain snow that stays high on top of the peak to release bubbling streams in spring that feed so many below. You can make a difference and a very big one, just like the snow on high peaks.

How do you prepare to avoid an avalanche at the end of your life? It is a cumulative effort and it takes continual work. The preparation is not every day but you should be aware, keeping a pulse on things and updating and revising as the seasons of your life change.

The first snow often does not stick. If you start and then put things back on your list of "to do", I suggest you start another list with just two planning tasks: writing a will and obtaining an executor.

Make it a priority; the snow is coming.

Tracks and Trails

The tracks are the people, firms or businesses that you need to identify to administer your estate. Recording information is integral; get comfortable with it.

The trail will indicate what you need to prepare along the journey. Once a trail is completed you should make a note of your time spent completing the task.

You are going to need to have the following names and numbers in place before your death in order for your Executor/Executrix to finalize your estate:

Track	Trail
Lawyer	Address
Power of Attorney	Documented by your Lawyer
Executor/Executrix	Named in your will
Certified Accountant	Past income tax returns
Financial Manager/ Bank	Location of all branches you deal with
Insurance Companies	Named & type of policies
Pension Provider	Name and identification numbers
Beneficiaries	Names and addresses
Funeral Home	Burial/Cremation
Burial place	Location, service, wake.

The Final Season of Two Friends

As Sami and I talked, we decided to prepare for that final season. It was the first of many discussions, inquiries and notes written. How did we begin? We started to question what to do, when, and how much we had to do before the final avalanche. You would think it should be as easy as putting wax on your skies before strapping on your boots to go.

Questions Sami asked were, "Where do I start?" "What kind of things do I need to do and why worry about them after I'm gone when it won't matter to me?" We were exploring new ground. Sami resisted with thoughts like – anyone can clean up the mess after the "avalanche". Actually "Anyone" can't; it takes a team of people.

We found out what our foundation steps should be. We were going to need a combination of personal information, a number of people and a secure storage place that others could access later. It sounded as if we were opening up his private life. In a way we were, but he didn't have anything to hide that I knew of at the time.

We remembered that first ski trail we groomed around the lake. The setting of the track made it easy for others to follow. We assumed this would be a similar process.

Sami was like me, an average person. We had both worked for many years, collecting and saving to get where we were when we began this process. It was comforting to see our accomplishments and daunting to decide what to do next. What to do with all the accumulation? "Nothing" would have been an easy response. We just wanted to enjoy our ski trails. Just as those ski trails and the snow banks around them were real and tangible, so was all the accumulated 'stuff' that formed Sami's estate.

The urge to enjoy the new snow skiing sometimes dominated our thoughts. We knew we needed to forget our gear and put our energy into deciding how to manage his estate. With each other's encouragement and guidance our preparations started. It wasn't hard. Sami and I started with simple steps. Here is what we did.

We went shopping for supplies. This is not to say that Sami didn't have a house full of office materials; it was a stalling tactic we often took before jobs we didn't really want to tackle. Our shopping list included notebooks, pens, paper file folders and a shredder. Why did we need a shredder? Like a dominant bull moose, Sami wasn't going to leave evidence of any weakness should we make a mistake.

I steered us to the stationary store where my friend's daughter worked. I figured Sherry would help us find the supplies and we'd be in and out in minutes. Of course I was dreaming; shopping with Sami was always a long experience.

Sherry met us at the entrance and after introductions Sami produced his list of wanted supplies. Who knew there were as many types of notebooks as there are trees in the forest? Sami picked five different ones and put them in the shopping cart.

We moved on to the pens. Sherry had noticed Sami's arthritic swollen hands. She skillfully maneuvered us to the "fat" pen section that would be easy for his fingers to hold. Two of each, black, blue and red pens were put into the cart.

File folders came in a box; no major decision had to be made. Next was the shredder and then we were done. The variety of shredders filled two shelves. We'd been in the store about forty minutes now and I could see it would be at least another forty before just the right shredder was selected. There would be no input from me; Sherry would charm him into the right choice.

She took two up to the front counter for a test run. Sherry used a small section of cash register tape to demonstrate the capabilities of each machine. Wanting to try, Sami reached for the role of tape. It flew out of his hand down to the floor and rolled along right through the legs of the lady waiting in line behind us. The lady was texting and oblivious to anything going on around her. Sami knelt down to grab the roll of tape lodged by her heel. The texting came to an abrupt halt, but not before the brim of Sami's hat touched the hem of her skirt.

An apology seems a lot more sincere when one is on one's knees. Sami charmed the lady and she even helped him stand up again. She picked up the roll of tape and added it to our cart. Demonstrating a guise of self-assurance Sami quickly paid for everything while Sherry bagged and carried the supplies out to the car.

I thought we were finished but no – we had the roll of cash register tape in the bag. Apparently we needed to go to the hardware store and find something to hold the roll of tape as if we had planned on buying it all along.

Sami was a handy guy and could build anything but I was thinking of all the tasks we should be doing rather than more shopping for supplies to build a tape holder. The stop was mercifully short. We found a paper towel holder that would suit the need. He bought it and we headed home to start the "prep the exec" process.

We made lists that included the following:

4. Lawyers, Accountants, Bankers – We listed the names of professionals who would complete some of the final tasks (lawyers, accountant, and bankers). We left space for other names of people who would help but who we had not met yet.

5. Numbers – We wrote down numbers that identified Sami, as well as those he used for all his financial transactions.

6. Assets – We listed the most important assets that he wanted to pass along when he was gone, like his financial investments, artwork, and vehicle, etc.

7. Beneficiaries – We listed people who were important to Sami, and who would be his beneficiaries.

We went over this list many times, adding telephone numbers or addresses and eventually creating four separate files.

In the end the first file related to money matters and contained the Power of Attorney papers. Later, Sami added the will behind the lawyer's name, address and phone number. Income tax returns for the past two years were attached to the accountant information. Bank investment summaries were attached to the banks financial planner. I added the probate papers to this file later.

Over time, we made copies of Sami's identification cards and put them in the second file with the list of these important numbers.

The third file had the serial numbers of the vehicle, identification signatures on the artwork and pictures of assets.

The forth file had a list of beneficiaries with their addresses. We also included specific items that some had already received and items that they would be receiving in the future.

The four files we started with did expand substantially in the end. Without the preparation we did together, the administration of the estate would have been much more difficult.

Tracks and Trails

You have to start somewhere, and pen and paper is a good place to start your trail. Remember, this is just the beginning. Just as Sami and I started, you should also get prepared. Remember the snow will come; your avalanche may not be that far away.

Track	Trail
Lawyers, Accountants, Bankers	List the names of professionals who can complete some of the final tasks.
	Leave extra space for names to be added down the line.
Numbers	Record numbers that identify you, as well as those used for all Financial transactions
Assets	List the most important assets that are to be passed along after your death, such as financial investments, artwork, and vehicle, etc.
Beneficiaries	People who are important to you, and who you would like to be your beneficiaries.

These four files will take greater shape as we move forward.

Four Files (File #1)

Four files are enough to get you started. Once you begin, you will gain your confidence, making it is easy to glide along as you continue working on your plan, writing things down as you go.

File number one contained "people – financial" information.

You need to select people you trust who will agree to get involved in the handling of your estate. The list of people will grow with time, much like the snow and ice of a precipice.

It is a real reality check; you worked hard to get "things", now you have to decide what to do with them. Human nature suggests a postponement which is why these tasks have been left undone until now. Don't forget the lessons of the animals. They don't take days off; instead, they constantly accumulate, feed, store food and prepare for the snow. The importance of your accumulated effort affects a great many others once the avalanche occurs. While those accumulations are what you call your estate, they will become either diamonds or weights to your Executor.

The first step to deal with is to ask the people who will clean up after the avalanche if they would become involved (their names go in File #1).

You do have an estate and therefore need to pick an Executor/Executrix – someone who understands your attachment to the things you laboured for and how important they are to you. This executor organizes your papers and delivers them to the appropriate people you selected to help dispose of your accumulations. It is someone who can keep the trails groomed because they have no use or need for your possessions yet know the value you placed on these items.

Who is that person? If you're like me and without children, then close friends come to mind. But, wait – my friends are close to the same age as I am and might die before me. Pick someone younger. This is not necessarily a good strategy as young people sometimes do die prematurely. Young people are working and busy with their own families and accumulating their own wealth. Will they have time and take care of everything? It is a tough decision, but after some thought it becomes evident who should act on your behalf. You will decide on someone to ask if they will agree to be your legal executor. Once you decide, it is also a good idea to add another person as back up. It's not necessary, but neither was that last pair of poles you bought at a garage sale to add to your collection.

Now that you have selected someone, you have to ask if they are willing to act on your behalf. When you ask this person if they will become your Executor, chances are they will say yes. Stop them right there. Tell them you'd like them to think about it before agreeing. After all, you have put years into building your estate. You want it handled by someone who knows what to do.

Your next question to them should be "Do you know what is involved in being an Executor?" Listen to their answer carefully; remember your job is to help them before you go.

There is information in many forms on media networks. Some of this material will help and some may not fit your circumstances. There is nothing better than experience. That being said, if your executor doesn't have any experience in this area, you can make it easier for them. How do you do that? Take simple small steps. Remember the avalanche? It didn't just happen. It took layers of snow, ice, powder snow, melted water freezing again, snow building up until the final day before the slide. It isn't difficult, just a little work on your part. Gather all the information they may need, before it is needed. You have done it before; that is why you have an estate and why you need an executor.

Talk with your executor a lot and put your discussions in writing, with two witnesses signing your notes. This will help with any legal issues so that everyone (and I mean everyone) knows what you wanted to happen when the slide comes. This can't be left for later, as you may need drugs and/or oxygen at the end of your life and you will not think coherently when you get to that stage.

Keep your notes in a place that you're executor knows of or better yet from time to time give you executor a copy of the notes. These notes become the precipice, a beautiful sight, especially to your novice executor.

The notes Sami and I made for the first file contained the following information.

We looked at the list of names we had made of people who would help with the cleanup after the slide. The names included the lawyer, executor, power of attorney, movers, house cleaners, funeral home directors, accountants and banks. We knew there would be others but their name could be added later.

All the names would be involved with the financial affairs of the estate. They would either be billing the estate for services or those people who would be determining and administering the division of the estate assets. This file would become the accounting file.

Names and Numbers (File # 2)

This second file should be about important names & numbers used by the estate.

Names

Now when you were born, you were given a name. Some first born children were given a series of names, often to please family members but also to identify them from others with the same name. My thought is those with three or more names must have been difficult births. I say this because teachers make you write your name in grade one and the more names you have to print, the longer it takes and the shorter the recess time outside. One classmate of mine who particularly liked recess wrote his nickname, which was short. New to town, the teacher didn't know the family so he wasn't corrected, the boy went all through school using that short nickname and enjoying those long recesses. He continued to use this nickname through adulthood. Near the end of his life, when he ended up in hospital, nurses and caregivers used his given names, no one knew who they were referring to.

Your executor needs to know your legal given name(s) so write them down. And remember, names change: sometimes by marriage, sometimes by choice. Your executor needs to know this as well: what the originals were and what the current legal names that identify you are. If your name was changed as a result of marriage then a marriage licence and number must be recorded.

Numbers

The government knows that names change but they do want taxes paid no matter what you call yourself. They are prepared. Right after birth you were issued a SIN (social insurance) number. This number has stayed with you from birth to death and is needed after you die when the estate is being settled.

The next number you need to record is your birth certificate registration. If you can't find your certificate, Service Canada in the province of your birth can help you. Your birth certificate tells where you were born. Even though some little towns no longer exist and you never even lived there, the executor will have to know where you were born. This doesn't make sense now, but trust me. In some municipalities, your executor can't get your death certificate without proof of your birth.

Medical

Importantly, the next numbers needed before your death are your medical insurance numbers. They will be referenced against bills after your death.

Attached to these numbers are "Plan" types or letters. These will help your Executor determine what bills can be claimed on income tax and which ones simply have to be paid.

Benefits – Pensions

We are lucky in Canada to receive benefits (which we pay for in a number of ways) from the Government.

Monthly cheques which you have been spending or perhaps saving also come with numbers that identify you. If you worked, you have been receiving the Canada Pension each month. After 65 you receive another pension from the government called Old Age Security. Another number (your social insurance number) is used for this pension.

A company and/or union pension plan can be paid out in various ways and your executor must know how that is done if you have been receiving a company pension. Record the name of the pension plan associated with your company pension.

Insurance

If you carry life insurance, write down the name of the insurance agent and once again the number of the policy.

Another benefit of living where we do is that we can enjoy that fresh fallen snow. Today seems like a good time to get out there and do just that. Take your executor with you so you can go over what you wrote down, answer their questions and decide where you two are going to store this information.

Strap on your snow shoes or cross country skis and enjoy the wilderness like you did as a kid. This time notice how much there is at the side of the trail: the shrubs, trees, rocks, snowdrifts. There are also many footprints in the snow; you have been making footprints all your life. Don't leave a chopped up icy path. Your executor will be counting on your clearly defined, smooth, and nicely groomed track in the future.

Tracks and Trails

Tracks	Trails
Your full legal name	Birth certificate number and copy
Social Insurance number	Copy of card
Medical Service Plan	Number and type of plan
Pension	Policy number, contact information
Insurance	Agent and policy type/coverage

Jack Frost – Executor and Power of Attorney (File #1)

You will wake up to Jack Frost on your window and white hoar frost on the mountain tops. Look at the window: the frost makes such beautiful patterns. Somehow, if you look closely, the crystals look like a forest, mountain peaks and valleys. Don't get upset that you didn't replace those windows with the energy efficient ones; if you had, you wouldn't see the frost. Put a towel on the window ledge, it will warm up, the frost will form little streams that will twist and turn on the way down, much like mountain streams high above.

As your window clears, you will notice fresh snow on the mountain top. Snow up there usually forms a number of layers. The first crystal layer is soft with a lot of water in it. If you make a snowball it will stick, water may drip out and it can get hard like an ice ball. With an icy layer on top, the cold goes down and the ground gets hard.

Like that wet ice layer forming under what will be your avalanche, mentally, the next step is harder. The step is determining a person to be your Power of Attorney. Having a POA is essential. This decision might leave you cold at first but an estate is all about your money. You may think otherwise but it is true. The cold hard fact is that your estate will eventually be about your money.

You think you'll spend it all before you go but it's not likely. When the cornice cracks, the slide comes fast and forcefully. You won't have time to make decisions, you won't be there to pay the bills and, most importantly, you can't take it with you.

Better stop, go out for coffee and spend some money now. Take your executor.

Your Power of Attorney and your executor might as well be the same person. It is easier that way, as you are only putting the information in one place. The Power of Attorney doesn't sign on and then go to your bank account and draw out money for some holiday in the Alps. You are still around and in control of your money. You just picked this executor and Power of Attorney because you know they are organized, care about you and are capable of handling your estate. They have agreed to ski that extra mile with and for you. They will act on your behalf when you can't negotiate financial transactions that you approve. You are still in control of your money; you are just using an assistant.

Financial numbers

There is another layer added to the cornice and more snowflakes coming. Your executor already has some of your very important identification numbers. The next numbers are your financial numbers. This may give you a chill, exposing your net financial worth. Well put on a scarf, and let's get this wrapped up; there are ski trails to explore.

Call your banker and tell them you want a spreadsheet listing all your assets, their account numbers and due dates. Go to the bank and go over the sheet carefully, make sure everything is there. Get copies.

The safe place

If you don't have a safety deposit box in joint names, yours and your Executors, maybe this is the time to do that while you're there. If you've decided to just use the metal box in your closet fine, just let your Executor know what decision you have made.

So far you should have completed the following preparation steps:

1. Chosen an Executor and a Power of Attorney (same person is suggested)

2. Recorded the important numbers that identify you and that are attached to your assets

3. Obtained financial statements from your bank and other investments

4. Decided on a safe place to store your written notes and statements

Remember that wet towel you put on the window ledge? Spread the towel out in your home. As it dries, it adds humidity to the room. You can breathe a little easier; nature has a way of taking care of you.

Tracks and Trails

Track	Trail
Power of Attorney	Legal document naming your selection
	Financial asset sheet
Safety deposit box	Location(s)
	Box number
	Key storage
	Names of those who have access

The Will and Possessions

Here are a few definitions to remember:

"Pinecone" – a relative who falls from the family tree, a result of greed and grasping for a larger share of the estate while ignoring the legal will.

Estate – the accumulation after years of shopping, spending, investing and saving.

Probate – the Provincial Supreme Court recognition of your will and your Executor.

Before writing your will, an inventory of your estate should be recorded. Starting with the big things is easy enough, but little things also have value so don't leave them out. When I refer to value I'm referring to the monetary assessment of that asset. Many possessions have emotional personal attachments, but those items can be dealt with later. The list you are making now would include the home, cottage, vehicle, diamonds and financial holdings. Anything that might not change or would increase in value in years to come should be listed. Things like your ski equipment, while valuable and essential to you, are really too small an item to list. You may not even have the same ones by the time the avalanche comes.

Don't forget you picked your Executor because they know your worth. Consult and listen to them when you are making your list. Some things you take for granted or have never considered may need to be added or removed.

Now that you have a preliminary picture of your estate and have discussed your findings with your Executor, it is time to write a last will and testament. Hire a lawyer do this for you using the information you provide him/her. There are two basic reasons to do so. First, you will be sure the will is legally binding. It will be registered, and there won't be a problem during Probate as to whether it is the one and only final will. Second, you will establish a relationship with someone you know. Should your Executor have a "pinecone" pop up and challenge the will, your lawyer will know what your true intent was when writing it.

Lawyers also know the fancy language that will hold up in court if it comes to that. It is surprising how many simple bequests in a will turn family members (pinecones) into people who think they know how much they deserve – how much they think they should receive – better than you. It all comes down to money; respect does not count, nor does the contribution they think they made to your life and happiness.

You've had years of accumulating your treasures and amassing your wealth. All of these things have meaning to you; they may have a value lower than you'd think, but are important none the less.

How do you write up a will with so much to consider? Again, it comes down to lists. If you had to move without anyone to help you pack and physically move, what would you take? I know it isn't realistic to expect someone at the end of their life to move alone, but it puts into perspective just what the most important assets you treasure are. Take a close look and think ten years down the road, assuming you live that long. Determine if the things you would have packed would still be treasures. You have been collecting for a long time and will continue to collect as we are people of habitual spending and accumulating.

The next list will be of the names of your beneficiaries. This should be your choice and yours alone. If you don't do things right, rest assured, there will be two beneficiaries you hadn't counted on. They are the lawyers, one for your Executor and one for the family pinecone.

Think of your beneficiaries and their current lifestyles. If you plan bequests to groups or organizations, what are their current positions and future needs? Ask yourself if your selected treasures would help, would be appreciated or would be as annoying as pinecones on your favourite ski trail. No matter how careful you are about selecting an asset for one individual, there will be problems. It is in peoples' nature, especially in families, to have one person want, demand or whine about some item another person received. You can't prepare for this but you can talk to your beneficiaries about your intended bequests. They probably will indicate your intentions are not necessary and don't fit their lifestyle. Perhaps they have difficulty talking about death especially of a family member. Don't be fooled. These individuals are being nice to you because they know there is money at stake. It is all about the money. They will wait and wait and your Executor will have to deal with them. Pinecones do drop on a nicely groomed trail.

So you select a lawyer to write up your last will and testament. You may not like to admit this but really it is the financial assets that will take precedence. Big ticket items like a home, cottage, motorhome, boat etc. will have to be evaluated after you are gone. Your will can stipulate whether these large ticket items are to be sold or not. Tell your Executor what your wishes are in this regard. He/she might have to arrange sales people and you might have some suggestions there.

You still have all that "stuff" – the important items you regard with sentiment and value you may wish to leave to a particular individual. You actually have two choices. Number one, give your treasure to them now. Unfortunately if you do that you can't continue to enjoy the item. Number two, keep the item and make a statement in your will indicating your bequest of the item to that particular person.

A few special items should be all you deal with, and if you put a particular part of your estate in your will, don't give it away without changing your will. Your Executor will get totally lost looking for something mentioned in the will that you gave away before you died.

I'm not saying don't give anything away, these are your things to do with as you please. Tell your lawyer, executor and beneficiaries when you do let some of your estate go to a beneficiary before your death.

O.K., the lawyer writes up your will which you sign. Your Executor and power of attorney also sign legal papers agreeing to act on your behalf. All of these signed legal documents get registered with the government and won't be needed again until the big slide.

You get copies of these documents and they should be put in that safe place agreed upon by you and your Executor. If that "safe place" was a safety deposit box at the bank it must be in joint names, yours and your Executor. Why? When you die, all your bank accounts, investments and safety deposit boxes are frozen. Your Executor needs to be able to get into that secure place to get all your legal documents.

Leaving the lawyers office, the will is under way. You think about your death. The avalanche after you're gone seems to be getting closer. Not really. It takes many layers of snow building, compressing, more building and wind. There is no wind today.

You have been through the first blanket of snow. That was deciding on a plan. The second layer was deciding on your Executor, and then came that wet sticky layer that is too hard to ski: your power of attorney (again, perhaps the same person). These beginnings are hard and took time; you should reward yourself for being so organized.

Many layers of snow and ice are appropriately named 'graupel'. This snow forms round heavy rimmed pellets that act as ball bearings during the slide. You are grappling with your layers now. People are hoarders, you included. I'm not telling you to get rid of things now, but to consider their future. The pressure is building up on the mountain top, but you are still in control down here. You have taken care of the names and numbers; your Executor, power of attorney and your lawyer is putting it all together for you.

Time for you to go ski a few laps around the lake. Call your Executor as they could probably use your company and the fresh air. Don't forget to spend some of your money on lunch. Treat your Executor, as they will more than make it up to you later when dealing with your estate.

Out of habit, you may have paid for lunch with a credit card. Hate to put you to work so soon after your exercise, but remember the numbers page you started. Well now you can add page 2 and list all your credit card numbers, association membership numbers, driver licence and passport numbers. There will probably be a whole page or more but write them all down.

Make some copies and put them in that safe spot with the other important papers.

Tracks and Trails

Estate assets	List of items
	Monetary receipts and warranties
	Pictures of valuables
Will	Copy obtained from Lawyer stored in safety deposit box
Beneficiaries	Names and addresses; Items and names matched
Credit cards	Types, numbers, expiry dates

Valuables (File # 3 & 4)

It's snowing again, cold and windy. Not a good day for skiing but there are other options to consider. Look around at your things. Maybe today is a good day to start that downsizing. Talk to your children first, if you have any. If not talk to those who you think you'd like to donate your valuables to. See if they value some of your treasures or is it just you who sees their worth. Some people tape names on the back of items that they would like certain people to receive when they die. You could do that today. Alternatively, if you are ready to part with something, you could send or deliver the item to that person and enjoy their delight and have a nice visit at the same time. Remember, if you listed an item in file number three then give it away before you die, be sure to remove that item from the list or make a note (witnessed) and put it in the file number four.

Another option which I highly recommend (even if in these days it seems old fashioned) is to write a few letters. The most valuable things in life are family and friends. These special people are going to miss you. Having a personal letter from you that they can hold, read and read again will help with their grief.

What would you say? You might start with what you feel was your greatest achievement. Follow this by how they fit into your life and what that meant to you. Remind them of special times you shared, the laughs you had and even how you made it through the tough times together. If it is one of your children you're writing to, include the hopes & dreams you have for them. Tell them what you like about their personality, achievements and choices they have made so far in their life. If you are old and wise, give them that last bit of parental advice you've been meaning to impart.

It's still snowing, so continue writing. Thank them for being available to you when you needed chores done and errands run. Include the fierce debates you enjoyed and the laughter after time went by and the topic wasn't important at all.

Share some of your childhood memories and what you recall of their childhoods that they may have forgotten. Putting your thoughts and memories down is as rewarding to you as it will be to those left behind. Start with the oldest child or oldest friend, and work down to the youngest. Get started now. Place these letters in file number four to be opened after you're gone. Be sure to put the person's name on the outside of the envelope so they go to the right individual.

What would you like them to know and remember? Your words will be important to them once you're gone.

Tracks and Trails

Downsize

Charities

Garage sale

Family & friends

Letters

Beneficiaries

Family

Friends

Executor

Lawyer

Money Counts

You won't spend all of your money and you can't take it with you. That being said, it is expensive to die. You will have the opportunity to spend some after you are gone. It goes like this.

Something just doesn't feel right. Off to the doctor who prescribes something, then to the pharmacy – money spent. Still not feeling right, actually feeling quite bad – ambulance ride to the hospital – bill to follow. When you are discharged, you probably will have a ride. No bill unpaid there.

Once home you may find you need some medical aides, walker, wheelchair, oxygen or renovations to your living area – more expenses. Another slip and back to the hospital in the ambulance, getting to know these guys. People using this emergency service go back and forth a few times. It costs every time.

People you were not in daily contact with but who were friends will want to know you died. An obituary in one or two papers is surprisingly expensive. You will want something nice said and perhaps a picture in the paper.

After you're gone, there might be a funeral with lunch provided. At the very least, there will be a wake or gathering in your memory. You say you have prepaid all this. That is fine but although you planned ahead, new taxes that were not originally charged will have to be paid to the funeral home.

You have arranged your plot but the family and friends will want a grave marker. Your ashes or body will have to be taken to the gravesite. If the site is some distance off there will be expenses to get there. There are fees to the city for the internment. This all costs money – more than you think.

Your Executor will have to pay moving cost for your belongings. Little things like transferring mail to the executor add up. House taxes or final bills relating to your residence and hospice need attending to. Your apartment will have to be rented and there will be cleaning costs. Cleaning was covered by your medical plan which stops upon your death. After the avalanche, you have no more coverage. The shampooing of carpets, cleaning drapes, painting walls etc., become estate expenses.

An accountant who prepares your final income tax needs to be paid. Then the lawyer who probates the will expects payment. Yes your estate will spend money to see you on your way, so put some aside. The bills will seem to snowball but your good executor will handle them, which is why you picked the person you did. Don't forget to put some money into your joint bank account with your Executor so that there is access to money for these bills.

Planning for the financial expenses of your death is not only considerate, but vital to minimizing conflicts among those handling your affairs. Yes, it costs money to die and lots of it. You actually do spend your money after you're gone.

Money counts. Set some aside to pay your way. Whether you're going up or down, it will cost a lot.

Tracks and Trails

The following tracks and trails are of expected expenses:

Medical	Pills, medical equipment, care aides
Information	Obituary
	Postage – notice of death announcements
	Forwarding mail to executor
	Thank you cards
Belongings	Moving company, cleaning staff
Housing	Final month's rent
	Real estate fees
Accountant	Final tax filing

Reflections

Snowmen – ghostly images of people made out of snowballs.

Snow angel – imprint in snow representing one who has passed but watches over you.

The sun is out creating diamond sparkles in the snow. You skied ahead of Buddy but something had caught your eye. An opening in the forest revealed three snowmen.

Your Executor catches up and you ponder the forms. One is larger than the others and has a familiar toque. You recognize the knitting of your late wife. The face is smiling, a branch that is shaped like a hockey stick rests against the form. The middle snowman has buttons for the eyes and mouth. A large spool of thread makes up the nose. Someone planned these sculptures. The third form is slightly shorter and pinecones are its adornments.

You are quiet and reflective, your Executor doesn't interrupt. Then you take off your scarf and wrap it around the middle form. As you look up you can see an imprint in the snow. It is a snow angel – perhaps an image of your late wife sharing this special place along the trail you are known to ski.

The sun seeps through the branches and sparkles like diamonds are all around the snow angel. Thinking of your family, you both ski on. On the drive home you remember the diamond and ruby ring you gave your wife. It was to go to your daughter but didn't.

It starts to snow, reminding you of the avalanche danger. You wonder how it can be so peaceful and beautiful before the slide. What will cause the slide to begin? What is the connection between the snow sculptures, your family and the slide?

Avalanches – Snowballs and Slabs

International classifications identify eleven different shapes for solid precipitation, snowflakes. As delicate as they are, together they have a force that can be deadly.

When the snow grains first fall they encounter a variety of temperatures, those in the air and those on the ground warmed by surface heat. The grains crystallize, link together and form beautiful snowflakes. The crystals are many shapes and sizes and compaction of the snow is determined by moisture within the crystal, wind and air temperature.

These delicate crystal snowflakes, dance, bounce and crash into each other. They link like a chorus line and stick together. With each snowfall a particular 'type' or combination of crystal sticks to the ground. Conditions such as wind & moisture vary within mountain ranges and differ with each snowfall. The sequencing of layers after each snowfall will determine the stability of the snowpack.

A layer of ground hoar may lower the temperature and become a good adhesive for the next slush or watery snow layer. Wet snow grains or graupel (sometimes called pellet snow) may be a third layer after an early winter snowfall. The next storm might deposit cold dry snow. The layering might be crusted as wind polishes the top surface. Eventually there will be a build-up of weak layers between cohesive ones.

There are two types of avalanches. A loose snow avalanche starts out like a snowball. It gathers more snowballs as it runs down the mountain. Eventually there are hundreds of large and small chunks descending.

The second type is a slab avalanche which starts when a large area of snow breaks loose and starts to slide all at once.

The loose snow avalanche looks insignificant as they start. They are dangerous yet beautiful to watch. They move down the track, eventually spreading out at the bottom or run out zone.

The slab avalanche is much more dramatic, destructive and disastrous to those caught near it. A crown fracture line occurs at the top of what will be a mass or slab of snow that will slide as one unit. A separation of cohesive snow will slide on a weak possibly wet layer which may be several inches or feet below. As the avalanche slides, it deposits blocks of compact snow along the way. At the height of the slide, clouds of snow "dust" are raised. The wind prevalent before and that caused by the slide creates deposits of snow blown to either side of the track. The weight of the slide takes down trees and anything in its path. The deposition or bottom resting area where the slide stops fills with debris brought down with destructive force.

Clean up after a slide takes time. The heavy equipment cleans the roadways if the slide covered them. The regrowth of the forest that was torn apart from the force and weight of the snow take much longer.

One's life has many layers. Like the snow grains building up on the mountain, during avalanche season, one's life experiences become layers of accumulated wealth over the years. You must figure out which type of slide you are leaving behind for others to clean up. Without meaning to, you will create a path of destruction. Like the voids left from the rocks and trees torn from their roots during the avalanche, you will also leave voids in the hearts of those you leave behind. They will heal, but they will be marked with scars.

Tracks and Trails

Letters	Review letters you wrote, make additions if necessary
Investments	Inspect each carefully. If an investment is in joint tenancy and/or right to survivorship, they will not be considered part of the estate that will be shared by those named in the will.
Lawyer	If you want all of your financial assets to form part of your estate you must write a letter and have it witnessed. You must indicate that all joint assets and right of survivorship are being held in trust by the individual who is jointly named on the asset.
Executor/executrix	A copy of the letter indicating how the financial assets are to be calculated before distribution goes in the safety deposit box. The figures in this letter are what your executor will use when they apply for probate.

The Slide – Death is Like an Avalanche

There have been small avalanches for Sami in the last few months. Trips to the hospital, short stays and back home again. The skis remain idle while we talk about one last ski around the trail.

The sun has been beating down on that cornice for days now. You are in Hospice and our time together is precious. We are all sad and want more time with you. At the same time, it is hard to see you weaken and struggle.

It snows outside; the weight is piling up on the mountain top. You wait for the slide you know is coming. There is pain and much frustration.

Family and friends are at your side, even the one who will become the pinecone shows up briefly. You talk to your Executor and give the o.k. to move your belongings and you discuss the money one last time. Everything seems in order. It will not be so. We both know that and are loath to discuss the inevitable pinecone, but we do.

You see the slide coming and wonder, will it be the snowball avalanche of organs shutting down one at a time? The massive stroke like the slab avalanche would seem more merciful.

The wind has started to blow. There is a crack behind the cornice. We don't hear it down here, maybe it is those who have gone before, telling you to hurry up and join them. Could be one or two days before the slide occurs.

It turns out to be four. You were always strong and wanted things your way and on your time.

As it turns out, your death came suddenly like the slab avalanche. The family (all but the pinecone) were caught by the swiftness of the event. Even though there was preparation by each friend and family member, the shock radiated from your passing.

The destruction of any avalanche only reveals itself later. Like the chunks of snow in the run out zone of an avalanche that must be dealt with, the finalizing of the estate looms.

The Executor – 4 Steps

I called my friend George "Sami" all these years. We saw each other or spoke to each other on the phone every day for the past ten years. Really, I listened mostly – boy that man could talk even when we were huffing and puffing around the ski trails.

We groomed many a trail and he groomed me to be his executor when he was gone. Our last visit was yesterday in Hospice where he had been for the past two weeks. We went over things one last time, although we both knew we had been through it all before.

The phone rang at 2:45 a.m. I dreaded answering this call. The news, Sami had taken his last slide. We started planning for this event ten years ago, yet it is still a shock that leaves me cold. I promised Sami I would be his executor and I knew I wouldn't sleep anymore, so I got up to assemble the papers I would need. We had made notes together and I had made lists of what to do which needed rereading. I notice the strength of Sami's handwriting on the first notes and for the first time notice the style had changed to shaky rounded forms on papers added later.

Sami received a company pension whose head office was in Eastern Canada.

My first step today will be to call them. I can do this early as there is a three hour time change and someone down there will be working already.

Hopefully no one else out West will be up and calling, tying up the lines so I have to listen to that awful music. It is 6 a.m. here and my call is put on hold. The music starts. It takes three more tries and finally I'm talking to a real person. I give her the news about Sami and his pension numbers. She gives me her condolences and promises to put a stop to next month's cheque.

Cancelling a pension may not have to be the first thing done but when everything else is closed and you have time zones to deal with, you might as well start there. Also when someone dies, even when you are in shock, getting started helps you move forward on your own. It begins the grieving and healing process.

Again I re-read my list of executor duties that must be performed to complete the administering of Sami's estate. Funeral home directors, bankers and lawyers have all been chosen. It should be a smooth glide on our carefully groomed track.

Out the door, skis left behind, my first step involves taking the urn with Sami's wife's ashes to the funeral home. They purchased a dual urn so they will be together forever. For such a small woman the urn and ashes sure are heavy, I can hardly lift them. Maybe it isn't the ashes that weigh so much – the urn is large and beautiful, of course. She always had good taste.

Once at the funeral, home I give the director the following:

The urn

The receipt for her cremation

Her death certificate

Their marriage certificate

Sami's prepaid receipt for his cremation

Sami's birth certificate.

The director goes over everything and assures me Sami's ashes will be joining those of his wife. I am to come back in 24 – 48 hours to get the urn and death certificates for Sami. They will issue two certificates. I'm told I can get more but they're $27.00 each. Two will be enough.

Up to hospice to pick up the few possessions Sami left behind. I do remember to take a small bag. My small bag fills quickly with the new housecoat I bought for him just last week. I'm about to leave when a volunteer reminds me to get the contents in the bathroom. Two of everything: bowls for the teeth, the teeth upper and lower; hearing aids, batteries for the hearing aids; two combs and a large and a small brush; a shaving mirror, blades and foam. The after shave and smelling bath salts were a surprise to me – that he would use these scented products but not as much as four little blue pills. Then I see the card addressed to me. Seems the pills were for me, to help me find a new ski partner when he was gone. How we would have laughed if he'd given me that gift one day earlier.

Carefully I pack up these necessities although who would use a second hand personal care item I'll never know. All items go to the recycling bin but that will be later.

I pull out of the Hospice parking lot and just as I get into traffic, a high pitched sound comes from the back seat. Can't ignore that terrible sound so I pull into someone's driveway. I get out scrambling around to the back seat to find the bag with the sound. I pull out that bag of Sami's possessions and a squealing hearing aide stops as it crashes to the floor and bounces out and under the car. I grab it, throw it back into the bag but not before the top set of false teeth go sliding on the ice down the drive towards the front door. A pleasant woman is standing in the doorway watching me run for the teeth, which by this time have lodged themselves in the snow bank.

We meet, greet, I think of the blue pills, and I'm out of there. What if she saw the card and pills Sami had put aside for me?

My next stop of the day is at the law office. The lawyer is informed of Sami's death. We discuss what papers I am to give him once I receive the death certificates. He tells me he's just heard the news of a large avalanche that came down in the early morning hours. A coincidence, I'm sure, but it fits that they would have their slide together, Sami and the avalanche. An appointment is made for us to meet when I have all the papers in hand.

The first four steps have been made. The pension cancelled, Sami's personal affects collected from Hospice, the urn delivered to the funeral home, and finally contact made with the lawyer.

Tracks and Trails

Funeral Home	Arrange cremation
Hospital/hospice	Collect final possessions (list contents taken)
	Obtain billing procedures
	Give instructions for future donations in deceased's name
Law office	Set up appointment with lawyer
	Take financial papers needed for probate

An Arduous Journey

A message from search and rescue is on the answering machine when I get home. My cabin is needed by the rescue team, so I'm out the door and heading up the mountain. It is always awe inspiring to see an avalanche before the cleanup and time is of the essence.

I arrive at the bottom of the slide and marvel at the clean break. The starting zone at the top is almost devoid of snow. Rock and clumps of snow have gouged a wide track and the run out zone is massive. The wind blast zone is a white veil. The airborne snow caused by the wind and the force of the slide has covered the forest on either side of the track. Branches and tree trunks are bent with the sudden weight of the snow. These same trees will go from being completely covered and damaged into their tall stately forms by spring thaw.

An emotionally and physically exhausting day ends, and I reflect on how Sami would have enjoyed the running around getting things done. The news of the avalanche, the race up the mountain to open the cabin, and the following quiet in the mountains after the slide would be exciting to him. The avalanche has left its mark.

Four stops each day to deal with the estate is my plan. The first stop today will be the Bank. The manager takes a copy of the Power of Attorney papers and the Executor documents. I try to open an estate account by transferring a small amount from Sami's funds. This will take time so I put some of my own money in to get the account started. I find out later this is a mistake. Bills of the estate must be paid by the estate protecting the Executor's own financial records.

A day later, the bank manager informs me that Sami's accounts were frozen four days ago. I explain he was still alive then and that shouldn't have happened. They then froze my new account with my money in it. Be careful who you deal with – not all banks are professional. No use talking to young bankers who do not help you. There is another way.

I then ask to empty the safety deposit boxes. Sami had two boxes, both joint: one with me and one with his son. I am allowed to go into the one joint with me. Even though I am the executor that represents Sami I am not allowed to open the second box. A list of the contents of the second box is to go to the lawyer handling the estate. I am told company policy is the reason I am not allowed to list the contents. I ask for the written company policy but it is not available.

Up to the lawyer's office and explain what had happened at the bank. The lawyer sends me back with a letter to the manager. I still am not allowed into the safety deposit box to list the contents. It seems that the bank staffs have decided they are the executors and trustees of the estate. I go back to the lawyer's office and inform them that the bank chooses to ignore the lawyer's letter. We decide to use an account with the law firm for bill paying. This service would have been free at the bank; it will cost the estate for the law firm's involvement in bill payments. I'm in no mood to fight some smart-aleck power hungry bankers. I've got a friend's estate to take care of, as promised. I'm also not about to stroke anyone's ego, especially if they think they knew Sami better than me. We then request Sami's financial assets be moved to the law firm. No bank involvement will be better in the long run and the law firm I know I can trust.

My cellphone rings and the funeral home informs me I can now pick up the ashes and the death certificates. When you pick these items up you sign a series of papers indicating what you have received. An employee carries the urn out for me and goes to the trunk of the car. This is a dilemma for me as Sami always rode shotgun, unless his wife was with us. If she was there then he rode in the middle of the backseat so he could keep his eye on the speedometer and do the backseat driving. Both were in the same box, so the only solution was to place both carefully in the backseat, with Sami's side in the middle and then securely strap the box in place.

My fourth stop of the day is at the Service Canada office. I am prepared with the following:

Death certificates

Social insurance number

Canada Pension number

Old age security number

The numbers are given to the agent so she can cancel the pensions. Next I apply for the Canada Pension Plan death benefit. This is a onetime refund that will go into the estate fund (at the law office – no banks for me).

Tracks and Trails

Bank	Obtain up to date list of financial assets
	Collect will and papers from safety deposit box
	Close safety deposit box
	Have all accounts transferred to law office
Lawyer	Set up an account for paying the deceased's bills
Funeral home	Arrange for service
	Go over burial or cremation and procedure to
	picking up the ashes
	Collect the death certificates.
Service Canada	Apply for the death benefit for the estate
	Cancel Canada Pension and Old Age Pension

Probate

Today we will start the probate process. I take the original copies of the death certificates to the law office as well as both wills. The reason I take both wills is because Sami was the executor for his wife but never finished the process, having died before the final taxes were done. Our lawyer's legal assistant makes me many copies of the death certificates. She keeps a copy for their files and instructs me on the importance of keeping the originals in a safe place. I have one and it is sure not at that bank.

Probate means the lawyer applies to the Supreme Court of your province to recognize the will, to confirm that the will was the last and only registered will. The court then gives the executor the right to proceed with the administration of the estate.

The lawyer and I go over the will line by line, and then we go over Sami's wife's will. I am the executor of her will as well since he has died. Each item is addressed; some of the bequests in her will were not made. His will is just starting so after the Probate papers return from the Supreme Court we can start to deal with his will.

On the way home I drop a "copy" of the death certificate at the bank. They try to have me use them for the estate bills and leave Sami's investments with them while the will is being settled. After driving 167.5 km today dealing with this estate, I'm in no mood for know-it-all bank employees.

I have one last thing to do today. I check to see if Sami's old apartment in the home is rented. It is not, so there won't be a refund. Seems sad to have the estate pay a month's rent when no one is there and there is a waiting list of people trying to get into this home.

Once home, I'd better get those ashes inside. Even though it is a cold day I'm sure the ashes are red hot – Sami, knowing the abuse I put up with at the bank and the excess fees that will come out of the estate because of them.

Anger wells up and I e-mail the head office of the bank with my complaint. My comments are forwarded to an ombudsman. A reply comes back with no apology; just "they were following policy". I am not told what that policy is or why a 'policy' was enacted when the client was still alive. Nor was I told why my bank account with my personal funds, set up to pay Sami's bills, was frozen for four working days.

One large asset of the estate is Sami's vehicle. Off to the car dealership where he purchased his vehicle. The Manager looks it over and then checks the service record. Records indicate the warranty period is over and that Sami never had the service done other than two oil changes. Lack of service would have cancelled any warranty that might have been needed. Every corner of the vehicle has a dint and there are scratches down both sides that have to be appraised.

I drive across town to the collision repair shop. It takes an hour and a half to assess the damage. The written assessment comes out to almost as much as the vehicle is worth and that doesn't include the damage inside. I'm asked how the vehicle could get in such rough shape so fast. "Well," I reply, "it belonged to an 88 year old and he would drive it into the curb or post or snow bank every time he had to park. When he backed up, he went until he hit whatever was behind him." Over time these little bumps became bigger and bigger. The side scratches likely came from the walkers and wheel chairs or shopping carts that Sami used. The inside carried his wife's wheel chair, our ski equipment and a myriad of boxes and bags. I'm told it doesn't take long for the scratches, dints and torn carpets to add up to a large repair bill.

I travel back to the lawyer's office with the assessment and the repair estimate in hand. The insurance on the vehicle has been in my name and I've been listed as the principle driver for the last five years. I decide, with the lawyers, not to fix the dints as the repair bill would have had to come out of the estate. I want to hold on to something of Sami's so I decide to purchase the vehicle from the estate. The lawyer draws up the papers and I buy the vehicle for the amount indicated by the dealership. It still runs, my skis fit in nicely and although it is scuffed and scarred on the outside, it runs and will take me and his spirit to the ski trail. Driving the vehicle brings back a flood of memories that are just too difficult for me. I don't ski today. After sticking a For Sale sign in the window, I drive home. The vehicle sits in my driveway for two weeks, looking at it brings more sorrow than joyful memories. A young couple who I've never met see my sign, test drive it and buy it in its current condition.

Tracks and Trails

Law office	Obtain copies of the death certificate with law firm seal
Wills	Lawyer contacts government to confirm the copy is the one and only final will
Financial papers	Review names on each asset, determine if they are joint tenant with right to survivorship of part of total estate assets
Letters	Check letters or notes to see if any assets will be kept out of the estate because of name on the asset. If the investments were held in trust then all of the finances are to be included in probate.
Bank	Drop off copy of the death certificate to the manager
Residence	Written termination notice to be given for residence
Assets	Obtain written estimate of large estate assets

Snow Angels

The sun is out and I know it will be hard but I have to do it. After packing a small lunch and just one thermos of coffee, I'm on my way. Stepping onto the trail alone for the first time, I ski along the tracks we made together. It is cool and crisp, snow diamonds shining on the sides of the trail. It is so quiet without Sami's constant chatter. I come to the snowmen that we noticed just 3 weeks ago. The toque on the tall form has fallen on the shoulder of the middle one. Skis come off and I put it back in place. Fixing Sami's scarf on the middle one I notice icicles on the pinecone form.

These three snowmen could represent Sami's three children. The oldest was a very good athlete when he was young. The snowman is built with broad shoulders and the tree limb resting on the side looks like a hockey stick. This form must represent his oldest son. He is grown now and the father of Sami's only granddaughters. This son sure was a help to Sami and his wife. Whenever they needed him, he would drop what he was doing and show up ready to do whatever was necessary to make them comfortable.

The middle form reminds me of his daughter. I remember Sami taking his scarf off and wrapping it carefully around the snowman. His daughter was very close to her mother and cared for her right to the end. She was also close to Sami, constantly running errands for him, seeing him every day.

The third form is smaller than the others and now leans away from the first two. I try to straighten it but it is frozen. This form reminds me of his youngest son, rarely around to help Sami. He was a trying person yet still part of Sami's family.

For some reason, I climb up to the snow angel. Laying down, I make another one beside the first, making sure the wings touch. On the climb down I notice a rose hip, deep red that will be the finishing touch. I pick the berry and climb back to the little snow angel and place it on the tip of the wing. Sami's wife always wore a ruby and diamond ring, it seemed appropriate to add the adornment to this little angel.

The Pinecone Shows Up

A mail truck is coming up the driveway. It is unusual, as I'm not expecting anything. Guessing it is a sympathy card as Sami has been gone a week now. I go out to meet the delivery man. No return address, I'm asked to sign indicating that I have received the letter. I sign, my curiosity increasing as I realize it is in fact a letter and not another card. The letter is from a lawyer representing the pinecone.

They say every family has someone who decides they are entitled to more than the will stipulates. They also usually think they hold rank and should be listened to while they try to bully other members of the family. They want the money they think they are entitled to right away.

The letter contains threats if I don't provide the information and cash immediately. At first I am upset. The timing of the letter is so close to the death I question their grief. The letter turns out to be the first of several I take to Sami's lawyer.

I am not a lawyer but Sami and I picked a good one and I'm sure he will know how to deal with such ridiculous demands. Dealing with a pinecone and the demands they impose will make the process of administering the estate longer and will also cost the estate more money, which affects all the beneficiaries. I'm told to be prepared. More of the tenacious requests will come from the pinecone and will have to be dealt with. This turns out to be true and the legal bills mount. One person's ego and greed turn into an absolute waste of time and money. Sami would not be impressed knowing the estate money is being eaten up by legal fees.

I call and set up an appointment with the lawyer to address the letter and its "threats, demands and time frames". A date is set for next week, ours is not his only case and we both know the money won't be distributed for months. The pinecone can wait!

I make it a telephone day and call and cancel all Sami's credit cards, medical plans and insurance policies. The driver's licence and passport need to be cancelled as well and so I take care to do so. Next are the club memberships. I decide to go down to the club, see the guys and have a toast to Sami after cancelling his membership.

Back home, I sort through the mail, separating Sami's bills that are now being forwarded to my home. I will have to take these to the lawyer when I meet with him next week and his office will pay them out of the estate. I write them all down, keeping track of the mounting expenses. I am surprised at how much it costs when you die.

I meet with the lawyer. The professional, polite response he prepares for the pinecone's first letter confirms he is the right person to handle the estate.

Tracks and Trails

Credit cards	Cancel, note date and confirmation numbers
Telephone, T.V.	Cancel
House hold services	Cancel
Post Office	Have the deceased's mail forwarded to your address
Identification documents	
Drivers licence	Cancel and return
Passport	Service Canada office cancels this
Medical	Cancel all private care personal as well as Provincial medical coverage
Lawyer	Keep them up to date by providing unpaid invoices as they arrive.

Arrangements

Sierra white seems to represent the snow covered mountains and therefore is my choice for the granite headstone. After e-mailing several companies for competitive prices, I communicate directly with the people who do most of the work for the city gravesite where Sami will rest. There are many things to consider from letter and number styles to names. Many friends called Sami by his nickname but his wife's name was not shortened. His brother and other family members referred to him by the initials of his given names. Who do you please, friends or family? I pick up the phone to call Sami and ask him what he wants, but halfway through dialing his number, I remember. Some days are harder than others when you grieve.

Time to make a decision, I go with his wife's full name and his initials as was his brother's choice. The mason tells me the names are too long to go side by side so we stack the family name on top in large letters with Sami's wife's name underneath, dates, and finally Sami's initials over his dates. The design is e-mailed to me for approval. It looks formal but nice so I place the order.

The ashes have to be interred. A plot was purchased years ago and waits. I have the number of the plot and call the city which is a 5 hour drive away to make the arrangements. The city staff is pleasant and I am informed I will have to give them a week's notice before I come down with the urn. We go over the costs.

Opening the hole for the urn costs how much? "I'll dig it myself" I said, "after all, I've planted trees." On no, that's a city staff job. By the way, same cost whether the hole is 2 feet down or 8 feet down. Then there is a fee for the liner. I don't know what a liner is so I agree. When I got there that liner was a Styrofoam cooler. I could have bought one for $1.25 and saved a fortune. They may not have seen us coming but they got us on that one. Next, a fee is charged for the city to place the stone.

Setting the stone needs to be done later. After all, once the hole is filled it will settle some. If I put that heavy stone down and it fell and dinted that nice urn Sami's wife picked out, she'd likely rise up and give it to me for being so clumsy. So I agree they can charge for setting the stone. Here's where praying can help some – you'd better pray it doesn't freeze and snow and they can't find the hole when it does come time to "set the stone". All you have to do is get it from the trunk of the car and rest it on the fake grass around the hole.

Now these grave markers are heavy but chances are good there will be someone young and happy to show off their arm strength and strong backs.

Roads in cemeteries apparently are not meant to get close to that expensive hole. Call the nephew again. God bless them for showing up after a Friday night, remind yourself to feed them. Don't be cheap. Everything is heavy and they earned it. You got to see youth at their best this morning, after all.

So the Urn's in the cooler in the expensive hole, the stone is on the fake grass, prayers are said and you look around. What a sight. No, not the landscape although it is a great view, and even quiet. Every little stone has some china ornament, picture in a frame, some plastic and some real flowers. You've donated all those things to the Salvation Army, so you have two choices, run back and pick up something that you donated or go buy flowers. There can be a problem with real flowers. My own Grandma had a visit from the police when she was 78 years old. Apparently she'd been taking the transit to the graveyard every day to get a nice bouquet of fresh flowers from the latest burial. She was sharing these lovely flowers with the 'friends' in the residence. She wasn't banned from the bus or the grave yard, just given a stern warning. Not heeding the authorities, she continued at night collecting flowers until she could no longer get around.

Off to the flower shop for a bouquet and back again, hoping they last for a few days.

Tracks and Trails

Mason	Check birth certificate for spelling of the name and correct birth/death dates. Select lettering and rock or plaque design. Order headstone after written quote is received
City	Arrange for internment Funeral times and requirements

Tax Returns (File #1)

The ski tracks are the first to melt as spring announces its arrival. Two other noticeable signs are last year's shrubs & grasses straightening and turning color. The old forest trees sport small buds on the ends of branches. Like these first two signs of spring, file number one holds the evidence of the past year's assets that now must be dealt with on the final tax return.

There are two envelopes in file number one. Receipts that are tax deductible are in one envelope, assets to be claimed are in the other. Income tax for the year of death must be taken to the accountant by the Executor for Sami.

I had cancelled the pensions and the T-slips were being forwarded to me. In the first file we had placed the tax returns for the past two years. I looked at those returns to see the deductions that were allowed in the past two years. Similar deductions for the year of death are likely if I can find receipts. I take another look at the income and interest statements to make sure that I have the documentation for all the pension income as well as any other income accrued during the year.

There will be no more snow or spring skiing. The only drifts left around our track are deposits pushed to the side by the grooming snowmobile. All is quiet.

The bills have stopped coming and all the receipts accounted for. Some of the receipts had been set aside by Sami as he knew they could be used as deductions when filing the final income tax. The medical receipts that were not covered under his plan have been included. Charity receipts are there, ready for the accountant.

The final T slips from the Provincial and Federal governments have arrived. The T slips for the pensions arrived today, so that is also added to the envelope for the accountant.

Again I look back at Sami's tax returns for the past two years. This review reminds me that I do not have a receipt for the interest gained from his investments. A quick trip into town to the Bank to get the receipts is made. While there, I obtain another copy of the statement showing the charge for the safety deposit box rental, which is another deduction on the tax form.

I call the accountant and arrange to deliver the items I have collected. He reminds me he will need a copy of the death certificate, will, probate papers, financial statement as well as the tax returns for the past two years.

The accountant will complete the current year's tax return. When that return comes back he requests a 'Tax Clearance certificate'. Form TX19 – A tax 'Clearance Certificate' certifies that all amounts the deceased is liable for have been paid. This certificate covers all the tax years up to the date of death.

He advises me not to pay out any money to the beneficiaries before the tax clearance certificate comes back. If I do give the beneficiaries money from the estate and there is a problem with the taxes, then I become liable. He tells me the return will take a minimum of six months to come back.

When the first tax return covering the year of death is filed, it will be another six months until the final tax clearance certificate returns. I can see the pinecone splitting open by the timeframe of the procedure. The government can't be rushed and the process must follow the legal process.

Once the personal tax clearance arrives the accountant must submit a T-3 trust return for the entire estate. A clearance certificate for the estate must also be obtained (another 6 month wait).

The accountant should issue a T-4 to the Executor if they plan to receive an executor fee. This fee can be up to 5% of the estate assets.

Tracks and Trails

Accountant	Deceased's tax return
	Filing the final return requires the following documents
	Death certificate
	Birth certificate (some provinces)
	Marriage certificate
	T slips (for pensions)
	Interest statements
	Receipts for tax deductions
	Proof of Probate
	List of distributed assets
	Estate tax return
	Clearance certificates for both tax returns.
	T-4 for Executor

The Division of Assets (File #4)

Although spring precedes the lovely warmth of summer, it can be a turbulent season. Dark clouds, wind and rain hammer new growth in the forest. Walking the trails Sami and I shared so many times brings back a flood of memories. As we walked we shared laughter, discussions, sometimes heated analysis of issues, always educating each other. Our voices echoed as we walked today; the silence is deafening.

Is it over yet? The tax clearance certificates are back and the financial assets are to be divided as stated in the will.

First an accounting of all bills paid and money added to the estate must be prepared by the lawyer. There are two more bills that have to be deducted from the estate. One is the legal bill and the other is a fee paid to me the executor. The executor fee is based on the amount of the estate and is a series of percentages depending on the size of the estate.

File number 4 has the list of names and addresses of the beneficiaries. Each one must be given a statement of the accounting that occurred during probate. A small amount of money will be held back in case the taxation department decides they made a mistake and more money is owed.

The account statement is then submitted to all the beneficiaries for their approval. Once everyone approves the statement the final money in the estate can be paid out and the account closed.

In a perfect world, the will of the deceased is followed and the financial assets are divided as specified in the will. I will not be able to follow Sami's will. The pinecone claims entitlement to more assets than were stated as his equal share of the will. He claims he was "requested" by the deceased to review past financial records. He further claims he was "gifted" a large portion of the estate. The will does not indicate this to be true but Sami cannot be asked what his intentions were or whether the claims by the pinecone are true.

Pinecones seem to be able to claim all sorts of lies that cannot be verified because the dead person either did not document the transactions carefully enough or the intent of the transaction is unclear to the executor. Solicitors rely on the honesty of people. Stories made up by a pinecone can either be believed, challenged in court or a compromise can be made.

The lawyer drafts up a statement for the division of assets. Two of the beneficiaries will not receive what is clearly specified in Sami's will. The pinecone shows no respect for Sami's good intentions and fair equal treatment of his children. I'm told this happens in many families.

I decide there is no point in taking the matter to court. A compromise is drafted; hopefully, the pinecone's greed won't be so great that the unequal division of assets favouring him will be enough.

If the compromise is accepted by the pinecone and the other beneficiaries, Sami's will can't be followed. It is a sad series of events.

- Four files are completed:

- Visits made to the people named in File #1.

- An accounting of expenses & financial numbers in File #2

- Selling & distributing assets listed in File #3

- Distributing the estate to the beneficiaries listed in File #4

Sami's affairs have been completed, the sadness is not so pronounced. I think back to our days sitting at the chrome kitchen table writing down Sami's important numbers. Sami wrote them down while I read out the numbers and spelled the names and addresses of policies. We shared sticky peanut butter and jam sandwiches, drank coffee with a drop or two of spirits and laughed at what the nutritionists would say. Perhaps if we'd listened to her, we'd have had more time together.

Sami said the seasons always change; so does the cycle of life. It's the slide that is the destructive part of life, the avalanche that hurts. Yet, the mark you leave is what counts. The animals will let you know what is coming. I look around and see the mark Sami has made.

The side track of the avalanche has also made its mark, but the forest is returning. The moose is ready to calf, the seasons have changed.

Tracks and Trails

Lawyer	Go over final accounting
	Receive your Executor fee
	Distribution of all assets takes place

Appendix – Professionals

File #1	Phone	e-mail address	notes
Law office			
Accountant			
Bank			
Hospital/ Hospice			
Funeral Home			
Service Canada			
City/Town (Burial site)			
Mason (headstone)			
Church			
Caterer			
Newspaper			
Insurance Company			
Pension Provider			

Bills – Refunds – Identification

File #2	Phone	e-mail address	notes
Birth certificate			
Social Insurance number			
Credit cards			
Bank investments			
Passport – Driver's license			
Post Office			
Club Memberships			
Florist			
Charity – Thrift stores			
Moving company			
Auction house			

Medical clinics			
Red Cross			
Hospice			

Assets

File #3

    Real Estate agent

    Land titles office

    Vehicle

    Art Work

    Jewellery

    Large furniture

    Heirlooms

    Misc

Beneficiaries

File #4

Family

Friends

Charities

Thrift stores

Bequests (institutions)

For Executor

Road report

Avalanche report

Ski resort

Travel agent

Anticipated or not, death comes to all and treasures of the estate must be distributed. Sami and Buddy are two outdoor enthusiasts. This is the step by step process they take as they prepare one to be Executor after the death of the other.

Buddy's task of distributing a lifetime of assets while dealing with his personal loss hits an unexpected wall of ice as grasping relatives interfere. Disrespecting the spirit of the legal will, one relative demands a greater share of the remaining assets which leads to serious and costly complications. The avalanche and aftermath detail events that occur while closing the estate.

Written notes of one's wishes, a legal will, and files of information are woven through the story of these two friends. Simple steps are incorporated in the telling of this tale. These are steps everyone should take to avoid an avalanche of events.

CPSIA information can be obtained at www.ICGtesting.com
Printed in the USA
LVOW06s1042150115

422720LV00001B/24/P

9 781460 237328